D1738225

ALONE

The Journeys of
Three Young Refugees

Written by PAUL TOM

Illustrated by MÉLANIE BAILLAIRGÉ

Translated by ARIELLE AARONSON

Groundwood Books
House of Anansi Press
Toronto / Berkeley

Published in English in Canada and the USA in 2023 by Groundwood Books
Text copyright © 2022 by Paul Tom
Illustrations copyright © 2022 by Mélanie Baillairgé
Translation copyright © 2023 by Arielle Aaronson
First published in French as *Seuls* copyright © 2022 by la courte échelle,
an imprint of Groupe d'édition la courte échelle inc.
Jacket design by Ariane Dray
English edition produced by Two Muses Publishing Services

Groundwood Books / House of Anansi Press
groundwoodbooks.com

We gratefully acknowledge the Government of Canada for their financial
support of our publishing program.

Alone is an adaptation of the documentary *Seuls*, produced by Picbois
Productions and broadcast on Télé-Québec.

With the participation of the Government of Canada
Avec la participation du gouvernement du Canada | Télé-Québec

Library and Archives Canada Cataloguing in Publication

Title: Alone : the journeys of three young refugees / written by Paul Tom ;
illustrated by Mélanie Baillairgé ; translated by Arielle Aaronson.
Other titles: Seuls. English
Names: Tom, Paul, author. | Baillairgé, Mélanie, illustrator. | Aaronson, Arielle,
translator. | adaptation of (work): Tom, Paul. Seuls (Documentary film)
Description: Translation of: Seuls. Adapted from the documentary film of
the same name.
Identifiers: Canadiana (print) 20220244804 | Canadiana (ebook)
20220244812 | ISBN 9781773069272(hardcover) | ISBN 9781773069289
(Kindle) | ISBN 9781773069296 (EPUB)
Subjects: LCSH: Unaccompanied refugee children—Canada—Biography—
Juvenile literature. | LCSH: Unaccompanied refugee children—Canada—
Juvenile literature. | LCSH: Refugee children—Canada—Biography—Juvenile
literature. | LCSH: Refugee children—Canada—Juvenile literature. |
LCGFT: Biographies. Classification: LCC HV640.4.C3 T66 2023 | DDC
j305.23086/914—dc23

The illustrations were created digitally.

Printed and bound in China

To the children who come here.
To the parents who stay there.

Imagine that you're going away.

Far, far away.

And neither of your parents will come with you.

That's what Afshin, Alain and Patricia are about to do.

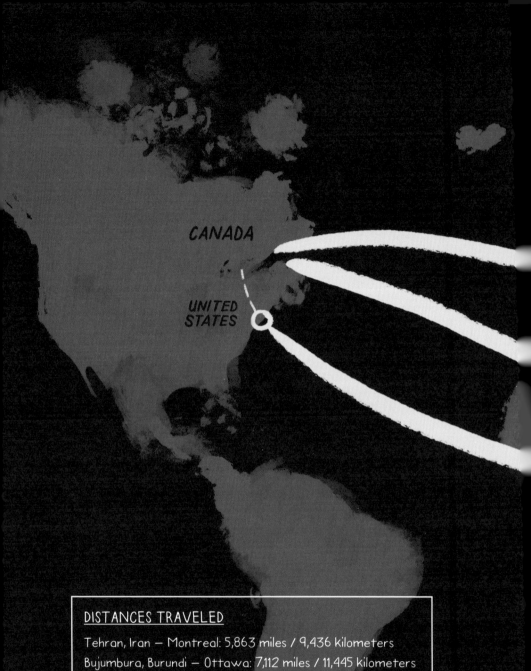

CANADA

UNITED
STATES

DISTANCES TRAVELED

Tehran, Iran — Montreal: 5,863 miles / 9,436 kilometers
Bujumbura, Burundi — Ottawa: 7,112 miles / 11,445 kilometers
Kampala, Uganda — Montreal: 6,981 miles / 11,235 kilometers

AFSHIN
13 years old
Tehran, Iran

ALAIN
13 years old
Bujumbura, Burundi

PATRICIA
16 years old
Kampala, Uganda

GREECE

IRAN

KENYA

UGANDA

BURUNDI

CHAPTER 1
Leaving Everything Behind

You have a family, friends, a home. You go to school, and like all children, you like to play.

One day, a threat appears and changes everything.

To escape the danger, you have to flee and leave everything behind, even though there are a thousand reasons to stay.

Your life will never be the same.

AFSHIN

My big brother and I love bugs. All kinds of bugs —
except cockroaches.

When I was five, my cousin put one down my pants.

I screamed, and I've hated them ever since.

In the summertime, we often sleep on the roof
because it gets too hot in our bedroom.

One night, streaks of light flicker across the sky.
Like fireworks. It's strange.

We can't believe our eyes. It's like a life-size version
of Star Wars!

And then suddenly ... BOOM! Bombs are exploding all around us. Everyone is scared.

Our country has been at war for years, but now the fighting has entered a new stage.

The war has reached our city.

The threat is hanging over our heads.

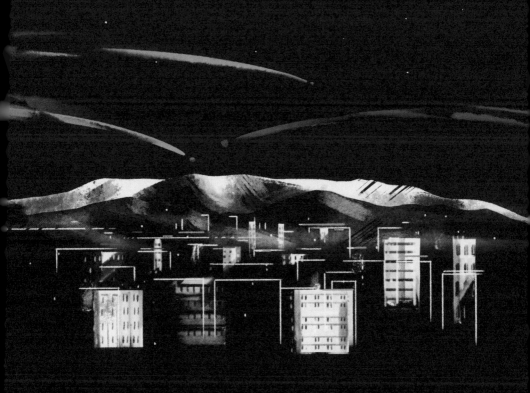

Now, every night sirens warn us that danger is approaching. We have to turn off all the lights because enemy planes can detect the smallest glimmer, even the glow of a cigarette.

We hide in the basement. My mother keeps repeating, "If we die, we die together."

Each time, we come out alive. Together.

Our family is the armor protecting us from war.

On TV, I watch the armies wage battle. Fighting a war seems so exciting. I want to be a part of it too! They say that soon I'll be old enough to be a soldier. I can't wait!

This isn't a game, Afshin! You can forget all about it!

I'm convinced that I'm a superhero. I'm invincible, and I'm not afraid of anything. Except cockroaches, of course.

My parents are worried. Unlike my brothers, who stay in line, I am reckless. My mother and father know that if I join the army, there's a good chance I'll run around like a headless chicken onto a minefield. And die.

My parents vow to do everything in their power to keep me alive. They think about my young cousins who went off to war.

And never returned.

Afshin, do you want to go on a trip?

Yes! When?

In three days. But you'll have to travel alone. Can you do that?

Of course! Where am I going?

My father takes out a map.

There. To Canada.

The only thing I know about this place is the Canada Dry ginger ale we sometimes drink.

Is it far, Dad?

Very far. Don't worry, we have everything arranged. But you can't tell anyone about it. Is that clear?

Aye aye, Captain!

I jump for joy. I've always wanted to travel!

"This isn't a vacation, Afshin. You're leaving for good. We might never see each other again."

In my excitement, I don't hear the anguish in my parents' voices. All I can think is, "Look out, world — adventure, here I come!"

Everything happens so quickly. It doesn't dawn on me that I only have three days left to live with them.

ALAIN

I am woken up by the rooster crowing.

It's better than the phone ringing. I hate when people call in the middle of the night. I jump every time.

My father is in the army, and he's often away on duty. I'm always scared that the phone will bring bad news. Two years ago, he came home with a bloody arm. The image is burned into my brain.

When I talk to my father, I can hear the machine guns firing and grenades exploding in the background.

When you grow up in Burundi, you learn to identify these sounds pretty quickly.

That's how it is when your father is in the army.

That's how it is when war is part of your daily life.

brrring   brrring

brrring   brrring

brrring

My two older brothers, Igor and Camille, have lots of friends in the neighborhood.

I'm more of a loner. I spend a lot of time with my mother. She's my best friend.

She's a businesswoman and she drives a car. That is rare in my country. She helps everyone: orphans, poor families, young students. It bothers me a bit, because it means she has less time for me.

One day after school, we hear on the radio that my father has been arrested.

... He's being held and questioned by the authorities.

They said Papa's name on the radio! How cool!

My brothers are worried. My mother is shaken.
She has to hold on to a chair to keep from falling over.
This is serious.

The authorities are keeping my father in some
sort of prison to scare him. Like in a nightmare.
Mama says some people stay there forever.
Some have even ...

Oh, no. I don't want to think about that.

Our days become very dark.

The phone rings often, but my father is never on the other end. Just faceless, threatening voices.

Mama gets letters with words like "kidnapping," "punishment" and "surveillance."

At night, shadows on motorcycles watch us and ride off in a deafening roar. I'm frightened. I can't sleep. I don't leave the house anymore.

"It's too dangerous here now. We have to leave!" my mother decides.

Nobody explains the details. They say I'm too young. I have no idea what the future holds, but Mama is there. I won't let her out of my sight.

Where are we going?

Are we taking a plane?

What about Papa???

PATRICIA

When I close my eyes, I see blue and green.

My country is full of lakes and forests. I love it when
the clouds cover the sky. I smell the first drops of rain
and I feel the calm before the storm.

The noisy city is a tangle of thirty-two dialects.
Once you move away from the commotion, it's peaceful.

I feel good. I feel better than I did before.

When I was little, I lived with my mother because my father had left us. My family believes that the firstborn must always be a boy. But I was born a girl, so my parents started fighting.

If I had been born a boy, would any of this have happened?

My mother and I lived in a shipping container. We were poor and constantly hungry, but we were happy together.

My mother always said,

One day, this will all be ancient history and we'll laugh about it.

Each morning, I would watch the other children run to school when the bell rang. They looked smart in their uniforms, surrounded by their friends. I watched with envy, because I had stopped going to class.

I had to work with my mother so that we could eat. We sold drinks she prepared herself. We walked a lot, but we were always together and we got to visit rich people's houses.

I dreamed about all that luxury and comfort. My mother liked to say, "If you want something enough, touch it and it will come to you." My fingertips would quietly graze the immaculate walls of those beautiful homes. I was convinced that one day, I would have access to all that wealth too.

We never became rich.

Because my mother didn't want to impose a life of poverty on me, she sent me to live with my father's sister.

A year later, she came back. She was waiting for me with a surprise. My father had returned and they were happy.

I still don't understand what happened between them during this time. Sometimes adults do things that remain a mystery to their children, even years later.

The important thing is that we were a normal family once again.

At sixteen, I sign up to play on a softball team.
It is a way for me to make new friends.

Without warning, my heart begins to beat wildly for
one of the other girls. I start feeling something that
I can't control. I've never experienced this before.
Is this what it means to fall in love?

The two of us spend more and more time alone.
When we're together, it feels like we're flying.
But we know we're playing with fire.

People say that it's unnatural, but how? What's unnatural about loving another person?

Whether or not we agree with what others think, we have to keep it a secret.

But the secret comes out.

My friend tells her mother, and her revelation goes off like a bomb. The news reaches my parents. They're horrified.

Even though they can't accept me for who I am, my parents want the best for me.

They know that if other people find out, it means prison and persecution for our family and even worse. It would be the end for me.

My parents will protect me.

As the news spreads, my parents decide that I have to leave quickly and go as far away as possible.

My mother calls my uncle in the United States and comes up with a story. She tells him that I have to travel to New York for a softball tournament and asks if I can stay with him.

My uncle agrees.

My father borrows money from the bank to pay for my trip.

I am holding my plane tickets. A round trip to America.

But my parents and I know that this will be a one-way trip.

CHAPTER 2
Saying Goodbye

The departure date is approaching.

You need to say goodbye to everyone you love and leave everything behind.

There's no going back. You have to keep moving forward at all costs, even though you have no way of knowing what tomorrow will bring or if you'll ever reach your destination.

AFSHIN

The night I'm supposed to leave, I go to a warehouse.

My mother holds me. She's crying so much she can scarcely breathe.

She hands me a red notebook.

I wrote down all of the advice a mother can give her son.

Mommmm!

You'll need it throughout your life.

What more advice can my mother give me?
She's repeated thousands of things already.

"Brush your teeth! Don't speak with your mouth full!
Don't tease your little brother!"

If you miss home, read the notebook. And you can cry. It's okay to cry.

Mommmm, you know that superheroes don't cry!

My son, my love. I can't believe this is the last time I'll see you.

My father gives some money to a man. He's the smuggler, the one who'll be taking me across the border. First to Turkey, then to Greece. I trace the route out on a map in my head. It's pretty far.

The smuggler opens the back door of a truck and points inside. It's dark.

"This is where you'll hide. Pile up some boxes around you so that nobody can see you."

I crouch down in the back of the truck, ready to play hide-and-seek. My mission is simple, stay invisible. Nobody can know I'm leaving my country to avoid military service.

Still, I know I would have made an excellent soldier.

I can see my parents through the boxes. They wave goodbye. I wave back. My mother is crushed by grief.

"It's time to go," says the smuggler.

BANG!
The door slams. I'm in complete darkness.

I use my flashlight to inspect the contents of my backpack: a sandwich, grapes, dried figs, nuts, a water bottle ... and a small pouch with 5,000 American dollars. I'm rich! Where did my parents ever find so much money?

We drive for a long time. I fall asleep.

Suddenly, the truck stops.

We're at a border crossing. I hear voices approaching.
They're searching the truck! I can't let them find me!
I squeeze my eyes shut, hold my breath and clutch
my bag.

The door opens. I repeat over and over in my head,

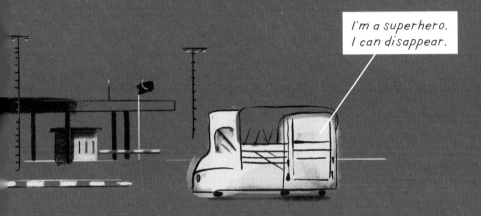

*I'm a superhero.
I can disappear.*

The door closes.
The border guards
didn't see me!
I let out the biggest
sigh of my life.

I finally arrive in Istanbul. I'm very stiff after spending more than thirty hours huddled in the back of the truck.

The smuggler brings me to a hotel.

"Don't move until I come back."

I open the door to my room. I'm terrified. There are cockroaches everywhere!

The toilet is disgusting, and drunk men are shouting at each other in the hallway.

I'm truly alone. The realization hits me like a slap in the face.

I look for a telephone so that I can shout, "Dad! Mom! I want to come home!"

But there's no phone. I can't call them.

Who will take care of me?

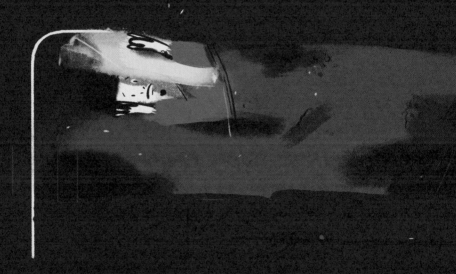

What am I doing here?

I cry all night long. Even superheroes break down
sometimes. I don't know if my mission will be a success.

The days go by, each one resembling the last.
I draw, I play solitaire, I count the hours and I sleep.

When I leave the hotel to find food, I always look for
landmarks. If I get lost, I can't ask a police officer
for help. I'm undocumented, I'm not supposed to be
in this country.

The never-ending days stretch out over a month.
I wait for the smuggler who never returns.

And then, finally!

The smuggler tells me that if I want to get into the West, it's better to come from a rich country. My new name is Marouf Alkhaiat and I'm sixteen instead of fourteen. In the picture, I'm wearing a white robe like the wealthy Saudi Arabian merchants. No trace of the little fourteen-year-old who won't be recruited by the Iranian army.

Onwards to Greece — one step closer to my goal!

The hardest part is behind me.

In Athens, I'm with other Iranians on the same journey.
We all dream of going to Canada. A boy says hello
to me. Now I have a friend. I won't have to be alone
anymore.

"In a week, you'll all be in Canada," the smuggler
tells us.

I still have $500 left. I celebrate with my new friend.
I don't keep track of what I spend.

La la la ...

Hey

hey

hey

Hey

hey

hey

La la la !

The week goes by. The smuggler tells us there has been a change of plans. We won't leave for another two weeks. Two more weeks?

"You ran out of money? That's not my problem. You should have been more careful!"

He shuts the door in my face.

I'm only fourteen and I've never had to manage a budget before.

I can hear my empty stomach protesting. I'm getting thinner by the minute. I'm ashamed, but I call my father. Money doesn't grow on trees.

My father uses his connections and the money arrives almost immediately. I'm lucky. Thank you, Dad. Thank you, Mom.

You're the real heroes.

Finally, the big day arrives.

The smuggler splits us into two groups.
My friend and I are in the second.

The first group leaves.

A few hours later, we hear they've been
arrested at the airport.

I look at my friend, terrified.

If we had been in that group,
we'd be in jail too!

The smuggler comes up with a new strategy.
We'll leave from a different airport.

The next day, we line up for passport control. I show
mine to the customs officer and he stamps it.
Victory!

The plane crosses the ocean. I go to the bathroom,
where I rip up my fake passport and flush it down
the toilet.

I'm fourteen-year-old Afshin again.

As the plane lands, I see the snow.
I don't even know the word for "blizzard" yet.

ALAIN

It's raining the day we leave. My brothers, mother and I flee the country without telling anyone. We have to make ourselves as invisible as possible to escape the people who want to hurt us.

Mama makes it clear that I have to say goodbye to my childhood home.

We take a flight to Kenya. From there, we'll fly to the United States once our immigration application has been approved.

At first, we settle into a nice apartment in a chic neighborhood of the capital, Nairobi.

"In a few weeks, we'll be in a country where we can live in peace," Mama tells us.

I think of my father in prison. It feels like we're abandoning him.

The weeks go by, but we don't hear from the United Nations High Commissioner for Refugees, the organization that processes asylum applications. We're not the only people hoping to move elsewhere.

Our money is running out. We have to move. One, two, three, four times. Each time, we find ourselves in a smaller, less comfortable apartment. We're getting poorer by the day.

My brothers and I have stopped going to school. In Kenya, you need money for school. At first, I think it's funny. I hang out with other kids who don't go to school. We play together, wander the streets, fool around. We're bored to tears.

I spend my time doing absolutely nothing. Waiting for I don't know what. I'm wasting my time.

✳

I was thirteen when I arrived in Kenya. Now I'm fifteen.

Mama, my brothers and I are now in our eighth apartment. If you can call it that.

Mama keeps telling us that our file is moving forward.

We have to keep our hopes up, it's only a matter of time.

I dream of bread and butter. Anything but lentil paste.

That's what we've eaten every day, twice a day, for three years.

You know Mama's doing her best, don't you, sweetie?

It's like living in a bad dream, day after day, for months.

As if our daily struggles weren't enough, my mother falls seriously ill. She goes to the hospital. She doesn't even have enough energy to talk.

63

On December 24, the phone rings. It startles me, like it used to when my father would call us from the field.

"Can you come to the hospital?"

My brothers and I take the bus.

It's the longest ride of my life.

My heart screams in silence the moment I see her.
Her condition has deteriorated so much that I hardly
recognize her.

I'm afraid. I don't dare imagine the worst. I can't.
Mama is a fighter. She's my hero. I still need her.

The doctor speaks to us in Swahili.
It isn't my language. But I understand
him perfectly.

MAMA?

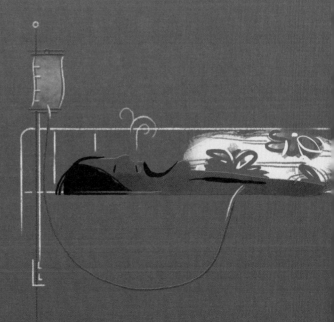

Your mother is dead.

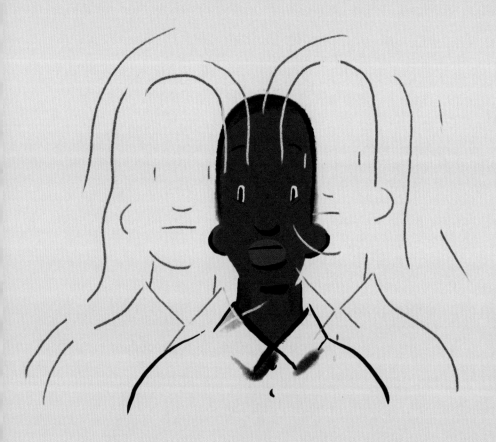

I can't breathe, I can't see, I can't remember where I am. My heart stops beating. I'm floating in space. My Mama, my compass, is gone. Nothing will ever be normal again.

At what age is it natural to lose your parents?

My brothers and I organize Mama's funeral.

Our mother buried here,
our father imprisoned there.
We are alone.

And we have nowhere to go.
We are lost.

                                        I am tired.

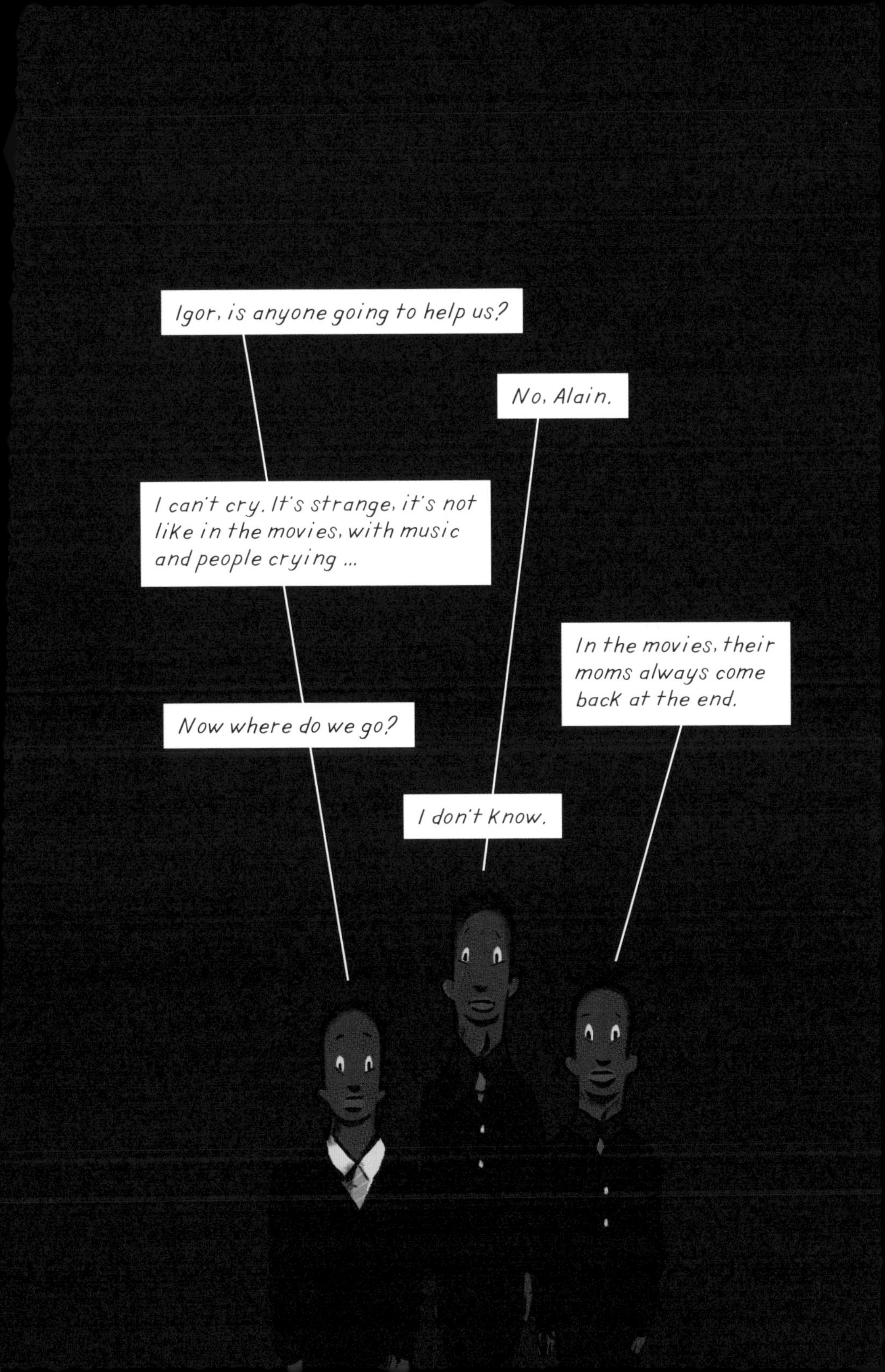

Igor, is anyone going to help us?
No, Alain.
I can't cry. It's strange, it's not like in the movies, with music and people crying ...
In the movies, their moms always come back at the end.
Now where do we go?
I don't know.

PATRICIA

There are three of us in the taxi that brings me to the airport: My mother, me and the silence around us.

In our stomachs, a dam holds back the tears.
It's steadfast. Neither my mother nor I fall apart.

My mother is a rock.
I take after her.

The time has come, but the clock seems to have stopped.
I don't realize that this is the last time I will feel the
enveloping weight of her love.

I walk toward passport control. I can't turn around or I will melt into a puddle on the floor.

I don't see my mother disappear behind me.

My feet move forward on their own. I mustn't make any mistakes.

This isn't the first time I've been in an airplane, but it's the first time fear has tied my stomach in knots the moment the wheels touch the ground.

I've arrived in the United States and I don't know what the future holds.

What's your name?

Where are you staying?

For how long?

Who paid for your ticket?

I'm at my uncle's house. He figures out there's no softball tournament. Caught off guard, he doesn't know how to help me. He's uncomfortable. And I don't like making people uncomfortable.

What time is the tournament?

Uhhhh ...

I decide to leave without telling him. I have two weeks to come up with a plan before the border guards and their sniffer dogs come after me.

This time, my mother isn't here to help me.

I do some research online. Canada seems to be the best place to seek asylum. I find a way to cross the border and I leave the day I'm supposed to return to Uganda. It's a big gamble.

HOW TO . . .

... cross the Canadian border?

I'm sorry, Uncle.

I take some money from my uncle to pay for the bus ticket.

I'll pay you back one day ...

The bus takes eight hours and brings me to a town near the Canadian border. My mind is blank. I'm a rock, like my mother.

Once I arrive, I ask for directions to Roxham Road. That's where asylum seekers cross into Canada.

I take a taxi. The woman behind the wheel warns me, "At the border, they'll tell you it's a crime to cross. That it's illegal. But don't let that stop you. Keep going!"

She's very direct. She says that Canada can't deny me entry. Requesting the protection of a country is a universal right. Universal means for me too. I'll be protected.

I take her word for it.

The border is up ahead, a few meters from the paved road.

I get out of the taxi.

I stand frozen in the middle of the road.

What if I go to prison? What if I'm mistreated? What if I never get out?

I lean forward. It's the only way I can get my body to start walking again.

The farther I go, the more I distance myself from my old life. I'm scared of the unknown stretching out before me. It's July, but I'm cold.

You'll have a better life.

I hear my mother's voice.
I close my eyes and keep going.

The moment I step onto Canadian soil, several police officers surround me.

I'm taken to Montreal, where I spend a few nights in a YMCA.

I send word to my uncle. "I'm fine. Don't come looking for me."

I delete everything from my phone and throw away all my ID cards, like in the spy movies. I've probably seen too many. I'm terrified that I will be chased down and identified.

I'm surrounded by lots of families looking for shelter just like me. A woman comes over.

"How old are you?"
"Seventeen."
"Where's your family?"
"I'm alone."

She is shocked into silence. Then her maternal instincts kick in and she quickly reassures me, "Don't worry. Everything will be fine. We'll look after you."

I hold back my tears. It feels good to know that someone is going to take care of me.

CHAPTER 3
It Isn't Over Yet

You've finally managed to reach Canada after risking your life.

You wish you could rest, but your journey is far from over.

Your path is still littered with obstacles.

AFSHIN

"Where's your passport?" is the first thing I hear once I get off the airplane.

My first hours in Canada are spent in an interrogation room. It feels endless. There's an interpreter with me, and English, French and Persian get mixed up together in my head. I don't know how many times I tell the same story.

"Yes, I'm alone. Yes, I took a truck, a bus and a plane. Yes, I left ten weeks ago."

Why don't they believe me? I'm too tired to go on. I just want to sleep, please ... it's Friday, and it's past midnight.

"You must report to this address on Monday. Do you have a place to sleep?"

Yes, I can stay with someone my father knows. I find my friend, who has been waiting for me for hours, and I call my father's contact.

"Do you know what time it is?"
"Yes, it's two in the morning. I'm really sorry."
"I can't come get you. Take the bus downtown. Call me once you get there."

Downtown? The bus? I'm already lost. Luckily, I have his address. We take a taxi.

When we get to the apartment, we
ring the doorbell and wait. A long time.
It's the middle of the night and it's cold.
What if nobody's home?

Finally, the door opens. The welcome
is icier than the temperature outside.
Neither my friend nor I want to stay,
but we have nowhere else to go.

I collapse with fatigue. In two days,
I'll be somewhere else.

At the Immigration Canada office, I'm already
exhausted at the thought of facing another
interrogation.

A social worker introduces himself.

"Hello, Afshin. My name is José DaCosta and it's my job
to look after minors who need protection."

Protection? I'm surprised by his gentle voice and
kind eyes.

"What types of things do you do for fun, Afshin?"

I'm not sure I understand the question. I ask the
interpreter to repeat it.

That's what I thought. He's asking me what I like to do.
Is he for real? Is this a trap?

I hesitate at first, but it feels like I can trust
Mr. DaCosta. I tell him about swimming, bugs,
my friends, my favorite foods.

Not once does he ask me why I left. I feel safe.

* Ghormeh sabzi is a traditional Iranian dish.

My foster family is Paul-Émile Lauzon.

He has a wonderfully kind face. He lost his wife years ago and he has an adult daughter who lives on her own.

The apartment has two bedrooms. Mr. Lauzon sleeps in the smaller one. The bigger one has four beds in it. I won't be alone. Other kids will be there with me.

The walls are filled with photos of Mr. Lauzon and different children at parties, restaurants, campsites and even on a trip to San Francisco! Everyone is smiling.

After an hour in his home, I'm smiling too.

Mr. Lauzon becomes Papa Lauzon.

ALAIN

We've just buried Mama in a cemetery in Nairobi.
We have to get four roommates to keep up with
the rent. We don't have a choice. There isn't enough
money. It's as if we need four people to fill the empty
space Mama left.

Mama is no longer there to plot our course or write
letters to the UNHCR.* We write our own letters
asking for help.

We don't know when our suffering will end and the
happy days will begin. I look all around me for a sign
that Mama is still with us. I search for hope in the sky
and in the trees.

Is there anyone out there who can help us?

* United Nations High
Commissioner for Refugees.

Ten months later — yes, ten months — hope finally arrives.

Hello, my name is Hugues.

Don't worry. Everything will work out.

I know what you're going through.
I lost my mother when I was young too.

What do you think about going to Canada?

Thanks to Hugues, we're granted an interview at the Canadian Embassy in Nairobi. We meet with a Canadian immigration representative and give a detailed account of the past three years.

I feel depleted after telling my story, but also like a burden has been lifted. The road ahead becomes brighter.

A few days later, the phone rings in celebration. Our asylum claim has been accepted! We're going to Canada!

Thank you, Hugues. For everything.

*

I still can't believe it. The airplane takes off. It makes me dizzy.

I look back one last time. At my home, my friends. The backdrop of my childhood.

Mama ...

I fall asleep whispering her name.

When I wake up, I see an immense sea of green through the window. Nobody told me that Canada was one giant forest! It's magnificent. Green gives me hope.

Igor, Camille! Look outside! It's beautiful!

Our feet touch down on the soil of a new country. We're welcomed with smiles. There's even a sign with our names on it. Someone is waiting for us!

"Welcome to your new life."

Mirjana, the social worker, comes with us to every appointment and helps us fill out a pile of paperwork. I've never signed so many documents and ID cards before. I think that's a good sign.

You'll live in a foster home for the next month.

Wow! This place is paradise!
Look, they're serving breakfast!
We haven't eaten breakfast in years!
And the menu changes at each meal! Morning, noon and night!
Camille, pinch me so I know I'm not dreaming!

PATRICIA

PRAIDA
Asylum Seekers

After the YMCA, PRAIDA* is next. Although I don't
know what all the letters stand for, there are kind
people who help me. PRAIDA is an organization that
supports asylum seekers like me.

They send me to live with Ms. Weber. She has been
looking after child refugees for years. I'm comfortable
in her home, but I like to be alone. And in three weeks,
I'll be eighteen. I'll be able to decide my future like
an adult.

What does it even mean to "become an adult?"

Fortunately, the social workers from PRAIDA are
there for me. They teach me to feel like less of
an outsider. With Ms. Weber, they help me find a
shared apartment.

* *Programme régional d'accueil et d'intégration des demandeurs d'asile.*
  (Regional Program for the Settlement and Integration of Asylum Seekers.)

I celebrate my eighteenth birthday with my future housemates.

They are also girls from East Africa and they arrived a year before me. They cook and sing. They're like a breath of fresh air. Together, we watch popular TV shows and laugh at all the same parts. It feels good.

My life is always changing. Every day brings new challenges, but I imagine that at some point, "it will all be ancient history."

"Now we can laugh about it," my mother tells me over the phone.

She's thrilled that I'm living with people who care about me. She's relieved that I'm safe.

Through my window, I can see snow falling for the first time. There's something magical about this burst of confetti marking a new chapter in my life.

CHAPTER 4
Mama, Where Are You?

You miss your parents.

Their hands on your shoulder when you're feeling unsure. Their beaming smiles when they're proud of you. The beating of their hearts against yours.

You miss your parents.

What else is there to say?

AFSHIN

It's the middle of winter and I'm going to school for the first time. I wear the snow pants I bought with Papa Lauzon the day before. I walk into the class for immigrants knowing only two words in French: yes and no. I don't understand a thing, but I try my best to answer.

Hello, is everything okay?

Yes.

Wow! You just arrived and you already understand French perfectly!

Yes.

You see, class, our new student just arrived and he already understands French perfectly. Bravo! What is your name?

Yes.

No, no ... W–H–A–T I–S Y–O–U–R N–A–M–E?

If it isn't yes, it must be no.

No, no, no, no.

Everyone bursts out laughing.

The teacher motions for me to sit down, then immediately holds me back.

"You have to take off your snow pants!" she tells me, pantomiming what she wants me to do.

What? Take off my pants in front of the whole class? No, no, no. Impossible. I can't do that. The teacher insists. I'm almost in tears. I run to the back of the classroom. I don't understand why she wants me to undress in front of everyone.

The bell rings. I watch in amazement as the other students get dressed to go play outside. What? The snow pants go on over the regular pants?

Note to self: tomorrow, wear underwear AND pants underneath my snowsuit.

After the class for immigrants, I get moved up to a regular class. It's hard because I don't speak French very well yet. I'm different. My hair, my clothes, my accent. I want to be like everybody else.

The boys around me all have girlfriends. I'd like a girlfriend too, but nobody notices me. I'm a grain of sand in the universe.

I hide in the library to eat my lunch. I read my mother's red notebook.

"My son, each moment is a gift. There is a light at the end of every tunnel, so never give up hope."

It's really dark in my tunnel. I don't know when I'll be able to see my parents again. Maybe one day my parents will come visit me here. But when? I have no idea.

In the meantime, I have the phone. It's comforting to hear my mother's voice.

"Afshin, you must understand that we sent you there so you would have a better future. Put all your energy into your studies. And stay away from drugs."

A mother is still a mother — even over 9,000 kilometers* away.

* 5,600 miles

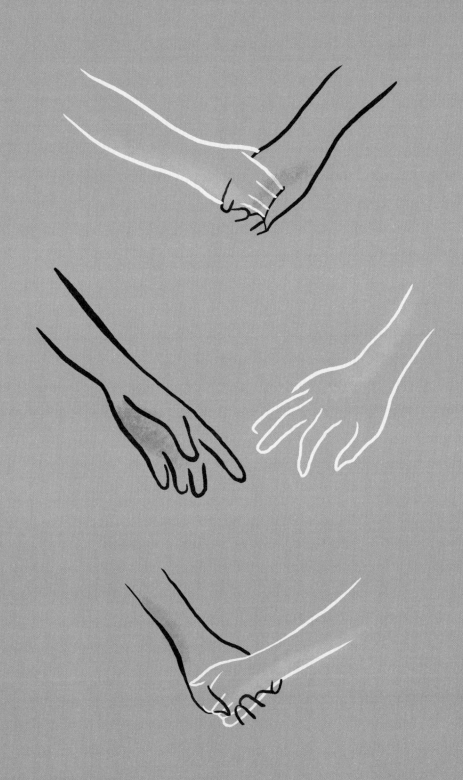

There are other Iranian students at school. At lunch, the food their mothers prepare for them makes my mouth water. I'm jealous. They were lucky and had the means to immigrate as a family.

One day, I'm invited to a classmate's house for dinner. On the table is ghormeh sabzi, my favorite dish as a child.

The smell brings back happy memories. I see familiar faces and I hear laughter, the sounds of children playing and adults talking loudly, carefree.

I take a bite. The world stops. I'm caught under a wave of emotions. My throat tightens. I start to tremble. It's so intense that I burst into tears.

At that moment, I can feel every kilometer separating me from my childhood and the people I love.

ALAIN

A month has passed. It's time to leave the foster home. The party is over.

My brother Igor was over eighteen when he arrived. An adult in the eyes of the law. It's his responsibility to take care of us. We move into an apartment and he works while Camille and I go to school. We have to send money to our father, who has been released from prison. Now he is the one who depends on us to live.

We're back in survival mode, like in Kenya. We try to manage our money, but it's difficult. When are you supposed to learn to make a budget and pay utility bills? And who knew we had to pay back our plane tickets? How do you cook for three hungry teenagers?

We manage. At least I don't have to eat lentils anymore.

Other kids my age go out and party. But not me. I have to work and study hard. I have some catching up to do if I want the same opportunities as them. I haven't been to school in over three years.

At the high school graduation ceremony, the other students are surrounded by their parents and loved ones. I pretend to look for my parents in the room. I know they're not there.

One morning, I wake up crying.

I try to stop, but I can't. I'm inconsolable. It's the first time I've cried since Mama died.

Do my brothers cry too? I don't know. We don't talk about these things. And we don't let anything show, either. Not our weaknesses or our emotions. We've been taught to stay strong.

But I'm tired of being strong all the time. I'm broken.

Mama is gone forever.

And I miss her so much.

I often dream of her.

PATRICIA

Winter arrives and shocks me to my core.

I only leave the house to go to work. The rest of the time I'm exhausted, as if I were a hundred years old.

I work in a warehouse, where I'm on my feet all day. My hands fly through the same motions, again and again. Everything happens too fast. It's eating me up inside. I have no energy left.

A colleague encourages me to go back to school.
Yes, when things get better, I'll go to school.
I'll learn French and make new friends.

For now, I just need to settle down and stop the clock.

I talk to my mother on the phone a lot. Her voice reminds me that we were together not so long ago. I feel like I'm growing up too quickly. I wish I were still a child, clinging to my mother.

I was prepared for many things when I came here. But not for a life without her.

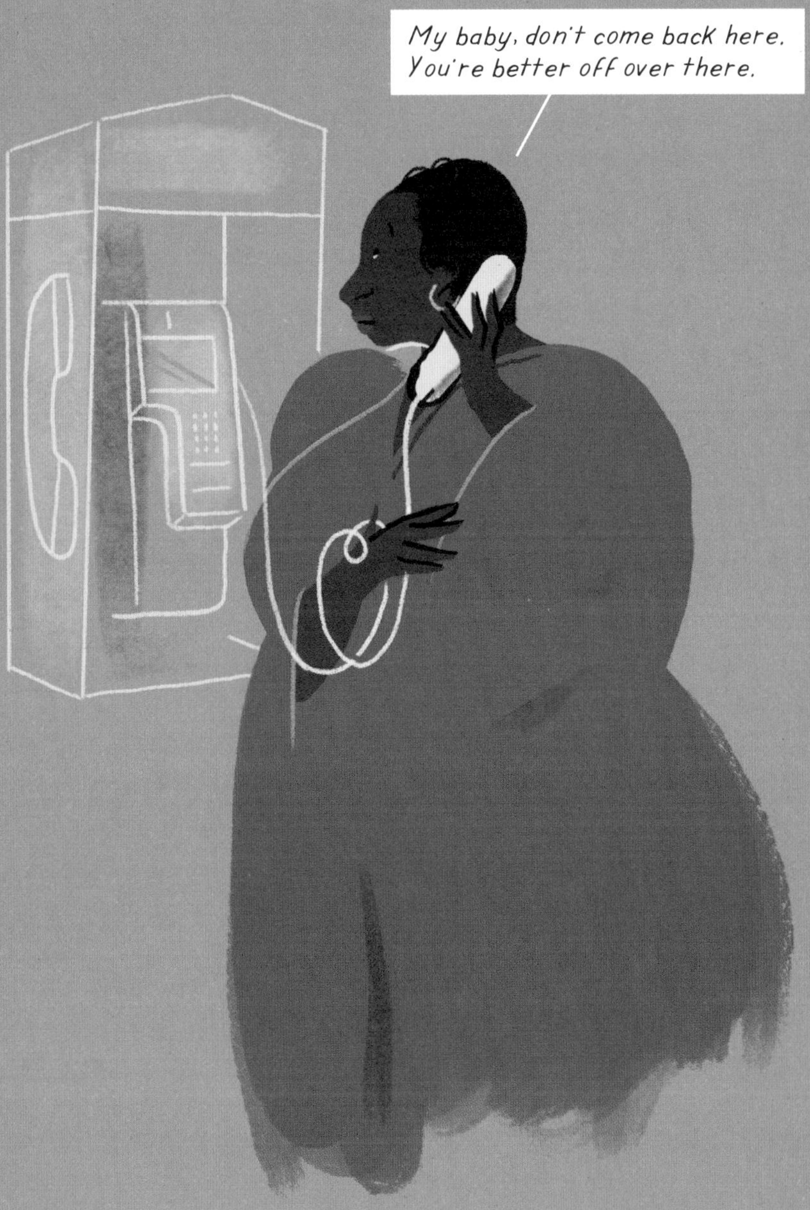
My baby, don't come back here. You're better off over there.

With my social worker, Vincent, I prepare for my hearing in front of the Immigration and Refugee Board of Canada. It's a major step. I'm going to go before a judge who will decide if I can stay — or if I should be sent back to my country.

Vincent has a bright, reassuring smile. He is happy to help me.

On the form, they ask: "Reason for departure."

I think about my friend back home, who I lost touch with, and everything that happened — the fear, the threats, the escape. I'm paralyzed by the memories, the trauma. The pain is still fresh in my body.

Once I heal, I'll tell my story to the world. If anyone is willing to listen.

For now, I leave the form blank.

I don't have the strength.

CHAPTER 5
Hope for Tomorrow

You've come a long way and braved many storms.

Tonight, the wind has finally calmed and the sky is painted with colors heralding better days ahead.

Now you can dream of your future.

AFSHIN

I'm lucky to have Papa Lauzon in my life. He looks after me as if I were his own son.

A phone call shatters the peace that is just beginning to settle over life. I must present my case in court, where the law will decide if I can stay in Canada or not. What do you mean, if I can stay? I've been here for two years ...

I answer the questions asked by the three judges in front of me. My lawyer isn't confident.

"There's a chance they'll send you back to Iran."

I see myself returning home to my parents in shame.

The judges stand to deliver their decision.
Papa Lauzon leaps up from his chair.

"I beg your pardon, Your Honors, but may I say something?"

Nobody can refuse a man with such a kind face.

My name is Paul-Émile Lauzon. Afshin has been living with me for two years. If you decide to send him back to Iran, it would be like taking away my own child.

Time stops. The judges talk amongst themselves.
I cling to Papa Lauzon as if my life depended on him.

I close my eyes and picture all of the times I've faced obstacles. At the border, when I could have been discovered in the truck. When I presented my fake passport to the authorities. Waving goodbye to the first group, which I could have been part of, and how they were arrested.

A person can gain or lose everything in a single day.

A judge turns to me. Racked with anguish,
I hang on his every word. He announces,
"Afshin, you can stay in Canada."

I jump for joy. Papa Lauzon hugs me.

Life is one big party.

ALAIN

After high school, I start thinking about my career.

My brothers are right. I run into roadblocks, the tests are expensive and I fail. Twice.

I need a change of scenery and to find another way to become a police officer, my dream job. I move to a different province more than 1,000 kilometers* away from my brothers. I want to join the army and gain experience.

This isn't the first detour I take, nor will it be the last. I'm not in a hurry anymore. I'm convinced my patience will be rewarded.

When I put on my military uniform for the first time, I think of my father. When he calls me from Rwanda, where he now lives as a refugee, I can tell that he's smiling. He believes in me.

I'm walking in his footsteps.

* 620 miles

I learn a lot in the army. I'm determined.

In my free time, I go to a church where I can gather my thoughts. There, I find a community that takes me under its wing. Scott is one of my new allies. He is a friend, a father, a confidant. His friendship comforts me.

I am confident. The stars are aligning. I can begin to dream again.

I want to become a police officer and help people in need. Start a family and bring my father to Canada. Return to Kenya and lay a bouquet of flowers on my mother's grave.

After the rainy season comes the sun.

Thank you, Mama, for
all that you did for us.
I'll never forget you.

PATRICIA

The date of my refugee hearing still hasn't been set.

While I wait, I write. It's probably the thing that makes me happiest. It's my work, and I get to decide everything. I'm in my own world. It's fantastic.

I also dream of becoming an actor. So that I can tell my story and bring people together.

I dream ...

... I dream of being free,

Of living in my own house.

I dream of seeing my parents happy.

I dream of going to a job interview without being ashamed of the color of my skin.

I want people to see me as a human being, not just as a Black person.

I want the world to accept me as someone who has hopes and dreams like everybody else.

I hope that one day, everyone will be able to go wherever they want without being afraid.

I dream that people will accept me.

And that I will accept myself.

— Patricia

I've woken up too early. Today is the day I have to go before the judge.

I hear Vincent telling me, "Remember, this is your story. You know the answers. You are the main character of your own life."

I take the form. Under the question "Reason for departure" I write, "I left because I was in love."

I am relieved to write these words. I feel that here, I have room to breathe. I feel protected. I feel free and safe. It was the right decision to come here.

To come home.

Each year, more than 400 children follow the same paths as Afshin, Alain and Patricia. They arrive in Canada alone, without their parents, to seek asylum.

There is a place for them here.

AFSHIN is in his fifties. He is married and has two children.

He works in a hospital as a radiology technician.

Six years after arriving in Canada, his mother finally came to visit.

"At the airport, I saw my mother. I ran into her arms. I breathed in her smell. I was a child again."

Afshin was so happy in Papa Lauzon's home that he stayed for eight years, even after he turned eighteen. Papa Lauzon has since passed away.

Some time after arriving in Canada, Afshin lost contact with the friend he'd met in Greece. Years later, by the magic of fate, Afshin ran into him again in the same apartment building where he was living with his wife, Maryam.

In his early thirties, he was able to return to Iran. Today, Afshin tells his story in schools using the autobiography he co-wrote, *Passeport pour ailleurs*.

For seven years, ALAIN pursued his dream of becoming a police officer while working as a social worker with street youth. At twenty-six, he became the first Canadian police officer of Burundian origin.

"This isn't just a victory for me, but for all young Burundians. It proves that anything is possible. I'm a first-generation immigrant. Others will be able to say, 'I can be a doctor.'"

In 2018, he went to visit his father, who lives as a refugee in Rwanda. Alain is currently trying to bring him to Canada. He hopes that one day, he and his brothers and father will be reunited in the same place.

Almost exactly two years after arriving, PATRICIA was officially declared a protected person in Canada and can now apply for permanent residency.

She came with a backpack containing almost nothing. Now when she moves, she needs a whole truck. She is slowly putting down roots.

She is in her twenties and wants to become a stuntwoman for action movies. She can live the life she wants, and her dreams change every month.

Here, that is possible.

The text on page 134 was written by Patricia herself.

Glossary

BORDERS: natural or imaginary lines delimiting countries or territories.

FORCED MIGRATION: involuntary immigration caused by circumstances such as war, natural disasters, persecution, poverty and more.

HOSPITALITY: the act of welcoming another person into your home and sharing a human connection.

IMMIGRATION: the action of moving from point A to point B with the intention of settling there on a long-term basis.

IRREGULAR MIGRANT: a migrant who has not yet been granted permission to remain in a country while awaiting refugee status.

PASSPORT AND VISA: documents required to legally cross a border.

REFUGEE: a person who has been granted asylum.

RIGHT OF ASYLUM: the right of every human being to seek refuge and protection in any country in the world, according to a convention signed by most countries.

SMUGGLER: a person who helps a migrant cross borders, often clandestinely.

UNACCOMPANIED MINOR: a child under the age of eighteen who is outside their country of origin without the presence and protection of a parent or guardian.

Acknowledgments

To Afshin, Alain and Patricia, for sharing all your time and emotions. Thank you for trusting me.

To Mélanie, for this straightforward collaboration and for your faith to move mountains.

To Mylène and Julie, for the hours of work you put in long before that evening in November 2017 when it all began. Thank you for this adventure, your talent and your friendship.

To the Picbois crew, Karine, Marie-Pierre, Catherine and Cindy, thank you for the strength, perseverance, vision and heart.

To Carole, for the invaluable support with this first experience.

To Brigitte, Alain, Alex, Marc-André, Samuel, Dominique, Pierre Yves, Ariane, Joannie, Fanny, Frédérique and Émilie, thank you for coming together to create what existed before this book.

To everyone who helped with *Bagages*, *Refuges* and *Pouvoir*, for your migration stories that inspire a world of words in my heart. To Mélissa and Nathalie, who are never far.

To my little flock, Danaé, Eve-Lyne, Caroline and Clara, for grounding me and for all your love.

To Papa, Mama and Madavine, thank you for being endless sources of inspiration, even in our silences.

— Paul Tom